Planting a Seedling

by Emma Huddleston

FOCUS READERS®

PIONEER

www.focusreaders.com

Focus Readers is distributed by North Star Editions:
sales@northstareditions.com | 888-417-0195

Produced for Focus Readers by Red Line Editorial.

Photographs ©: Shutterstock Images, cover, 1, 15; iStockphoto, 4, 7, 8, 11, 12, 16, 19, 21

Library of Congress Cataloging-in-Publication Data
Names: Huddleston, Emma, author.
Title: Planting a seedling / by Emma Huddleston.
Description: Lake Elmo, MN : Focus Readers, [2021] | Series: Life skills |
    Includes index. | Audience: Grades 2-3
Identifiers: LCCN 2019060218 (print) | LCCN 2019060219 (ebook) | ISBN
    9781644933459 (hardcover) | ISBN 9781644934210 (paperback) | ISBN
    9781644935736 (pdf) | ISBN 9781644934975 (ebook)
Subjects: LCSH: Seedlings--Transplanting--Juvenile literature. | Planting
    (Plant culture)--Juvenile literature.
Classification: LCC SB121 .H83 2021 (print) | LCC SB121 (ebook) | DDC
    631.5/2--dc23
LC record available at https://lccn.loc.gov/2019060218
LC ebook record available at https://lccn.loc.gov/2019060219

Printed in the United States of America
Mankato, MN
082020

About the Author

Emma Huddleston lives in the Twin Cities with her husband. She enjoys writing children's books and reading novels.

Table of Contents

Chapter 1

Seedlings

A short **stem** rises out of the soil. Small leaves grow off the sides. A seedling is a young plant. It has just **sprouted** from a seed.

People can grow plants from seeds. But they can also plant seedlings instead. People can buy seedlings at stores. Some seedlings are just a few inches tall. Others are more than 1 foot (0.3 m) tall.

Fun Fact

Acorns are seeds that grow into oak trees.

Chapter 2

Moving Outside

People can plant seedlings in pots or in the ground. But people must not move seedlings outside too soon. If they do, the seedlings may die.

Count the seedling's leaves. Look for four or more **mature** leaves. The seedling is now ready to live outside.

Leaves take in **energy** from sunlight. Plants use that energy to make food. Having mature leaves will help the seedling survive outside.

Life Cycle of a Lemon Tree

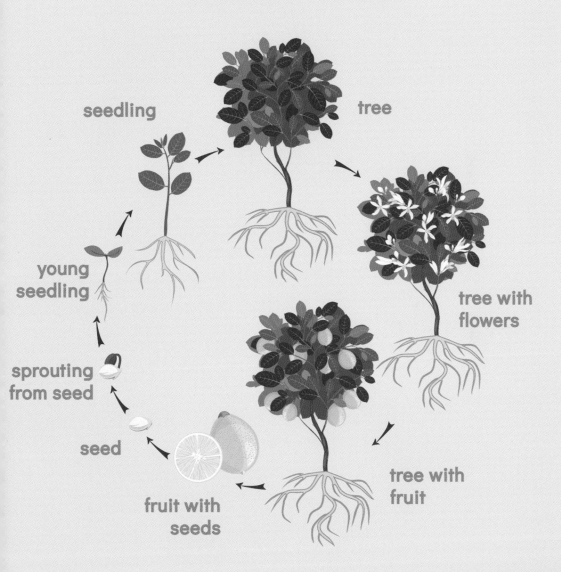

seedling

tree

tree with flowers

young seedling

sprouting from seed

seed

fruit with seeds

tree with fruit

Chapter 3

Planting in Soil

First, dig a hole. You can use a shovel or your fingers. The size of the hole depends on the size of the seedling.

Be gentle when you place the seedling into the hole. Fill the hole with loose soil. A seedling can't grow well if its roots are **cramped**. Soil should lightly cover the roots of the seedling. Don't cover the stem.

Chapter 4

Sunlight and Water

Plants need sunlight and water to grow. They also need healthy soil. Plants get **nutrients** from the soil.

Check on your seedling every day. Touch the soil to see if it is wet or dry. **Moist** soil is good. Dry soil is a sign the seedling needs water.

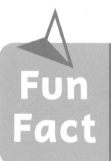

Fun Fact

Many tree seedlings need to be watered every 7 to 10 days.

Grow a Plant

Choose a plant to grow. Find the seedling at a store. Then pick a place with lots of sunlight. Dig a hole in the soil. Place the seedling into the hole. Fill the hole around the seedling with soil. Water the plant every few days. Watch your plant grow over time!

FOCUS ON
Planting a Seedling

Write your answers on a separate piece of paper.

1. Write a letter to a friend explaining how to plant a seedling.

2. What kind of plant would you want to grow? Why?

3. What do all plants need to grow?
    A. water, sunlight, and nutrients
    B. water, nutrients, and tightly packed soil
    C. sunlight, a shovel, and a pot

4. Why do plants need sunlight?
    A. Sunlight dries out the soil.
    B. Sunlight helps people see the plants growing.
    C. Sunlight gives plants energy to grow.

Answer key on page 24.

Glossary

cramped
In a tight space.

energy
The ability to do work.

mature
Fully grown.

moist
A little wet or damp.

nutrients
Things that people, animals, and plants need to stay healthy.

sprouted
Started to grow.

stem
The main body of a plant.

To Learn More

BOOKS

Dunn, Mary R. *An Apple Tree's Life Cycle*. North Mankato, MN: Capstone Press, 2018.

Hansen, Grace. *Seeds*. Minneapolis: Abdo Kids, 2016.

NOTE TO EDUCATORS

Visit **www.focusreaders.com** to find lesson plans, activities, links, and other resources related to this title.

Index

Answer Key: 1. Answers will vary; **2.** Answers will vary; **3.** A; **4.** C